UNCOMMON FAVOR

TERESA JOHNSON

Mission Possible Press, USA
Extraordinary Living Series

The Mission is Possible.
Sharing love and wisdom for the young and "the young at heart,"
expanding minds, restoring kindness through good thoughts, feelings, and attitudes is our intent. May you thrive and be good in all you are and all you do...
Be Cause U.R. Absolute Good!

"Be Encouraged, Uncommon Favor" by Teresa Johnson.

2025 Second Printing

Copyright © 2013 Teresa Johnson. All rights reserved. No part of this book may be reproduced in any form, stored in a retrieval system, or transmitted, in any form or by any means – electronic, mechanical, photocopying, recording, or otherwise—without prior written permission from the publisher.

Published by Mission Possible Press
A Division of Absolute Good
P.O. Box 8039, St. Louis, MO 63156

ISBN 978-0-9852760-5-8

Dedication

I dedicate these poems to God, for it is God alone who has given me the ability to write poetry. I have been blessed to capture my thoughts on paper, and God has allowed them to be used to encourage me and to remind me that I walk by faith and not by sight.

To all those who feel as if you are all alone in your troubles, be encouraged; and to those who know you are not alone, may these poems be a reminder during those times when knowing just doesn't seem to be enough. To my parents, Marvin and Beatrice, my brother, Marvin Jr., and his wife, Ann. My sisters, Dorothy and Deborah, and my beloved son, Antoine, his wife, Casey, and my darling granddaughters, Kayla and Peyton, I thank God for all of you.

To all my family and friends, thank you for your support.

To Friendly Temple and Hopewell MBC, my extended family, may God bless you.

And, as always, to God be the glory.

Contents

Foreword
Dr. Donald Ray McNeal, J.D., D.Min.

Introduction

PIECE ONE
Be Encouraged
LAMENTATIONS,
LOVE AND THE GOOD LORD
~1~

PIECE TWO
Just My Thoughts
CONCERN, CONSIDERATION,
THE GOOD LORD IS OUR CONSTANT HELP
~53~

PIECE THREE
Spiritual Poems for Life
LETTING THE GOOD LORD BE,
THANK YOU GOD
~95~

About the Author
~115~

Foreword

I rejoice in the privilege of writing this foreword for The Reverend Teresa Johnson's anthology of poems. Be Encouraged, Uncommon Favor, is a rich array of poems and prose presentations about varied subjects that are quite human, common and yet worthy of reflection, dialogue and learned appreciation. Each poem is short enough to provoke an agreeing thought from the reader; and yet, deep enough to invite their mental dialogue in the subject being discussed. I walked away from the laments as a believer seeking "the deep things of God and Christ."

Teresa is bent on trust through the unfaithful challenges, which come each and every time, we declare a faithful trust. Certain poems speak of sustaining places (moments) surrounded by hurt and heartache. As a male, the emotional struggles were awkward to me, but as a pastor I know the truth behind them, having ministered to so many women who are growing professionally.

While others remind me of Aristotle's dialectics, "I do not need, then I do need." I was lifted through great word; and the announcement that Jesus Christ offers perfect insight. Well said. Well explored.

The most inviting to me was "Feelings," as the fluidly to the human psyche;; here, "life's conquest" and "your job to keep your feelings in control" speak to an awareness that the person has a part to play in how long and how deep the feelings take us. I was inspired by this poem especially. Personal cravings can cause a search for a cure that is synthetic and then a cure that is a spiritual "remedy." The discovery that the Lord made a way, left the journey as solved, but from a high power. As I saw Teresa probe for Ordination as a Missionary Baptist Minister at the Hopewell Missionary Baptist Church, little did I know the Lord had launched her to the literary forefront of publishing. I know her to be a worshipper and these poems confirmed it. The prose contrasts are superb. The thesis of each poem is clear, and the resolution of the problem offered a fresh, learned approach that only a few can give. My prayers for this present work and inspiration to do more go with you.

Dr. Donald Ray McNeal, J.D., D.Min.
Pastor, Hopewell Missionary Baptist Church

Saint Louis, Missouri, Spring 2013

Introduction

Writing poems is away in which I can release some of the pressures of everyday life. Poetry allows me to say on paper what I'm feeling inside. I then can ask myself questions like, why am I feeling this way, and is there anything that I can feel grateful for while in this state of mind? And the answer is always yes, realizing that all things work together for the good of those who love the Lord and are called according to His purpose and plan.

It is my prayer that we the people of God will begin to walk in the power and dominion that He has given us as born again believers. It is only when we begin to understand that the trials and hardships, as well as those great and glorious times in our lives are all set up to allow us to grow into the person(s) whom God has called us to be. Those are the times that we get to take on the traits and character of our God.

A songwriter once said that there are only two times to praise the Lord, and that is when you feel like it and when you don't. So, no matter what has taken place in your life, God is always worthy to be praised. Hopefully, these poems will be encouraging and a blessing to all those who read them.

Love,
Teresa

PIECE ONE

Be Encouraged

LAMENTATIONS, LOVE AND THE GOOD LORD

Be Encouraged

Be Encouaged..4
In This State of Mind..4
I Can't Stop Now..5
It's a New Day..7
Shake It Off..7
Trust...9
Why Does My Spirit Cry?...9
Let's Take This Time..10
When I...10
I'm in Love with Heaven Above...................................11
My Special Place..12
God's Love...12
Just Think..13
Someone Like Me...14
Let Thy Will Be Done..14
Without God..15
Worship..16
Just...16
I'm Sure...17
Morning..17
My Angels..18
I Just Need You..18
Lord, I Need a Word..19
Don't Complain...20
Lord, You Always Come Through................................20
I Praise...21
I Must Confess...21
Have You Ever?..22
I Know I'm Blessed..23
Weeping for a Night...24
In a Little While...25

Rest a Bit	25
Lord, What I Want to Be	26
You're Amazing	27
Come, Holy Spirit	27
Let's Worship	28
God Won't Forsake You	29
It's All Right	29
A Soul's Story	30
Rhythm of Life	31
I See God	32
Here I Sit	33
He's a Keeper	34
Open Eyes	35
Let Go and Let God	35
A Talk with the Lord	36
The Goodness of the Lord	37
God's Favor	38
To Be Used by God	38
Not Just Another Day	39
It's the Season	40
My Special Valentine	41
December Anew	41
Happy	42
Entering In	43
Storm	43
Pray, Pray, Pray	44
Faith Revealed	45
Under the Sky	45
Satan Can't Stop My Praise	46
An Unfamiliar Place	47
Somewhere	47
Our Mother and Friend	48
They're Gone	49
Sunshine	50
Fifty	50
Uncommon Favor	51

Be Encouraged

I have lived on this earth for more than forty years, and in all that time, I've shed many tears.

I've seen loved ones come, and I've seen them go. I've been at the verge of losing my soul.

But God and all His power and strength lifted me up and blessed me with His wisdom and some common sense, for God has always been my defense.

At times, things have been hard, at times, things have been good, and there have been times that I have been misunderstood.

But through it all, I can only say that God keeps on making a way out of no way.

And if there were something special that I could share, it would be to tell you that there's much power in your prayer.

In This State of Mind

In this state of mind that I'm in, my heart is heavy, and I feel like I don't have one real friend.

I can't define this state of mind.
My thoughts are dark, and I feel so alone.

I wake up crying, "God, please take me home."

Help me, Lord, while I'm in this state;; I'm tired of not knowing my rightful place.

I'm being attacked on every end, but I know I must trust in you, Lord, and depend.

I depend on your words and your wisdom to show me my end.

I know I'm not alone in this state.

There are many others in this world who believe that they can't win this rat race.

But I have a word from the Lord.

Stand still and wait, trust in the word of God and have faith, for the God we serve never makes a mistake, although this state seems to be unfair,

God has chosen to allow us to be taken there.
So, don't concentrate on the state, but praise God for keeping you safe.

And just know that while you are in this state that Jesus has already taken your place.

I Can't Stop Now

What in the world is going on?

My whole world seems to be falling apart.

I need you to help me, Lord.

What in the world is taking place?

I just don't see a way for my escape.
What am I to believe?

Is this the way it's supposed to be – struggling to make it in life?

Please – this can't be right!

I don't know how much more I can take.

I'm so sick and tired of my life being in such a devastating state.

I stand out most of the time, yet I am that one who seems to be left behind.

I talk a lot about my God, you see, and because nothing seems to be happening that the people of this world can see, it's like I'm a red dot in a black sea.

But I try to put on the strength of the Lord,
Yet sometimes, I just don't have the heart.

Does that make me weak? No! I don't think...

It just makes me have to seek the will of God before I can have real rest or peace.

So, come on, all of you who are just like me; get back on your feet. Shake yourself off and began to speak.

Speak into the atmosphere, letting the world know that God placed you here. And that He owns your mind, heart, body and soul.
Here we stand with power, strength and might because Jesus has already won the fight!

He died and rose on that third day, walking with all power in His hands, and it's our job to praise Him and say amen.

You can't stop now;; Jesus gave up too much for us to act as if we don't understand.

All power is in His hand, and He alone is the reason why we all can stand.

It's a New Day

In the morning when I rise, I open my eyes to a glorious surprise, for God has allowed me grace to be alive.

As the day starts to unfold, I'll try my best to reach God's goals and plans for my life – it's only right since He gave the perfect sacrifice.

I'll pray for love, hope and peace;; I'll pray that God use me to be His mouthpiece.

Although there is a lot to be done, with the Lord on your side, the battle has already been won.

It's up to you and me, you see, to make sure that we bless the Lord and be vessels that the entire world can see, that the God we serve is the best that there will ever be.

Shake It Off

I know things seem to be out of hand, and nothing seems to be going as planned.

But pick yourself up, and shake it off. God will never leave you in the dark.

I know you do all you can to stay in God's will, yet sometimes, you feel so unfulfilled; You need to pick yourself up and shake it off.

Stay in the race no matter the cost.

I know it looks like you are all alone.

When you need someone to talk to, there's no one at home.

You need to go ahead and shake it off.

Open up your mouth and speak, for God hears and knows what you want to say before you can even speak.

I know sometimes you are confused about what it is you were called to do.

And you know God has spoken a word over your life, but you doubt if you can get it right.

You need to shake it off and stay in the fight because when God speaks, it's already all right.

So, no matter what's going on, you have the power to be strong.

God picked you up and shook you off; He stopped you from being lost.

He gave a direct command for your life, and it's up to you to stay and get it right.

So, whatever comes into your life, learn to stand up and shake it off and fight.

Trust

I must trust in the Lord and not in what I see.
I will trust in God's word and believe that I am able to achieve whatever God has for me.

I will trust in the power of love and what it can do when one loves with a heart that is true.

I will trust in the hope that God has given me, letting me know that I am free.

Free from the doubt that comes from shame when I think back on how I used to live before I knew Jesus' name.

I will trust in peace as I seek to do those things that normally make me weak, but because I trust in the Lord, there will be no great defeat, as long as I trust in the God of love, hope and peace.

Why Does My Spirit Cry?

Why does my spirit cry?

Is it because of the way I see life out of a spiritual eye, watching as the people of God living life beneath their means, not standing up and fighting for anything?

My spirit is hurting deep down within;; I can't believe all of the sin that we have allowed to creep in.

My spirit cries when it sees how the house of the Lord has become some kind of rehearsed scene.

We've learned how to pick the time to give a shout, then throw our heads back and pass out.

My spirit cries while looking all around, watching as our children are falling down.

There are not enough holy role models around to help them stand their ground.

Why must my spirit cry?

When Jesus lived and died just so you and I could stay alive and walk in his Holy gift of love and righteousness?

Let's Take This Time

Let's take this time and make it great just by blessing

God and having faith.

Let's take this time and celebrate God's mercy and grace.

Let's take this time and rejoice, knowing that we are no longer lost in a world full of sin because Jesus' blood has adopted us in.

Let's take this time and pray for God just keep on making a way, for He is God and God alone,
and He took the time to leave His throne just to show us the way home.

When I

When I got to know you, I got to know me.

When I learned to trust you, I learned I could trust me.

When I found hope in you, I found there was hope for me.

When I trusted in your perfect peace, I learned it was not always necessary to speak.

When you showed me your mercy and grace, I knew you would always make a way for me to escape.

Escape from the wages of sin so that I could live again.

But when you gave me your love, I knew I was blessed from heaven above.

I'm in Love with Heaven Above

I'm in love with heaven above, in love with the stars on high,

In love with the dark blue sky,

In love with the ocean and sea, in love with God's cool breeze,

In love with the trees, in love with the colors of all the different leaves,

In love with life because of God's great sacrifice,

In love, you see, with the fact that God chose me,

Chose me just the way that I am with all my faults and having no love, just seeking my own way of trying to stay above,

In love with God's helping hand, in love with all His divine plans,

In love with life, you see, because God has delivered me.

My Special Place

There's a special place where I can go to get rest from all my worldly thoughts of woe.

In this place, I am at peace with the thoughts of Jesus

Christ as my shepherd, and I'm His sheep.

As He takes His rod and His staff, guiding me on the right path, there is nothing else sweeter than Jesus being my teacher.

With my head bowed down at His feet, looking up only when He speaks,

For in my special place, I am complete just to sit and hear God speak,

Complete to be His loving queen and able to share God's love for all human beings.

I can feel His hand as He touches the crown, the crown of my head as I bow down.

With one touch from Him, you see, I began to worship and praise Him continuously,

Because in my special place, you see, there's only God and me.

God's Love

Oh, Lord, how wonderful is thy name.

Oh, Lord, your love never changes.

Just like in the days of old, you still care about your people's souls.

You open doors that no man can shut.

You are the only one who really forgives and forgets.

You, Lord, love with a love that is true.

You have kept your promise to see us through.

Know, Lord, there is none like you, a faithful and loving Lord.

Yes, it's true, and I thank God for you.

Just Think

I remember when there was no you and me,

But it was you only loving and keeping me.

I remember how you held my hand,

Never letting me stray too far away from your plan.

I think about how you walked this earth as a man, spreading the word of God throughout the land.

I think about your great sacrifice, how you laid down your life,

And when I think about all these things, I thank God for sending us the perfect King.

Someone Like Me

Who would have ever believed that someone like me would walk in my destiny?

Someone like me would have the mind to believe that God has already delivered me?

And now I am free to be the best that I can be and to achieve all the goals and plans that God ordained for me.

Yes, someone as unlikely as me now knows what real love is supposed to be.

Just because God above gave up His only begotten son to come and give me grace.

He didn't even care about all of my past mistakes.

Oh yes, He took someone like me, trusted and believed that I could go and do good deeds,

And if God has that much confidence in me, I'm glad that He could use someone like me.

Let Thy Will Be Done

'Let thy will be done' is what's in my heart, although sometimes I don't act the part.

'Let thy will be done' is the way it must be if I am to serve thee.

Let thy will be done so that I can be the best person I can be.

Let thy will be done over me so that you can use someone like me.

Let thy will be done so all the world can see that there's no other stronger and mightier God besides thee.

Thy will has to be done if we are to portray the image of thy darling son, for it was He who set the pace and gave us a way to escape the wages of sin, and for that, we praise his Holy name and say amen.

Without God

Without God, there would be no light of day, just dark clouds of gray.

Without God, there would be no birds, grass or seeds, and never would there be a cool breeze.

Without God, there would be no human life, no need for Jesus to make a sacrifice.

Without God, there would be no love or hope, just doubt and despair filling the atmosphere.

But we are thankful, for we have a God,

One who never leaves our side, one who stands mighty and tall, one who gave His all that we might have a chance at life to be free from misery and strife. He is our God, our God alone, and He will always be on the throne.

Worship

The heart of a worshipper is one that is pure, one who praises God with a love that is sincere.

To be a true worshipper of the Lord, one must ask God to touch their heart.

One must worship in the good times as well as the bad because no one can praise the Lord and remain sad.

A true worshipper understands that the joy that they have did not come from man, but it comes from God's divine hand.

The heart of a worshipper believes in the fact that with God, there is never any lack.

The heart of a worshipper is one that prays and always thanks God for a brand new day.

To be a true worshipper, you see, is to praise God continuously.

Just

Just a closer walk with thee,
Just as close as close can be,
Just a word, a word from thee,
Just one word is all I need.

Just a touch, a touch from thee,
Just one touch will set me free.
Just a smile, a smile from thee,
Just a smile will strengthen me.
Lord, just your love, your love is all I need.

I'm Sure

Just as sure as God is above,

That's how sure I am of His love.

It's His love that brings me through when so many times
I don't know what to do.

And when I feel like all hope is gone,
I can hear Him saying, "My child, just hold on, for
there's no need to get upset.

Just stand back and let me bless.

I bless your comings and your goings,
I bless you in your not knowing, for I am God and God
alone.

Trust in me and be strong, for just as sure as heaven is
above, I, God, am love."

Morning

In the morning when you rise, what is the first thing you
do when you open your eyes?

In the noon of the day, wouldn't it be nice to take the
time and pray?

In the evening when the sun is going down,

Take this time to thank God for keeping you around.

And when you lay your head down for a good night's
rest, know without a doubt you are blessed.

My Angels

Angels in my midst, taking care of my prayer list.

Angels in my midst, fighting, making sure that I am fit.

Angels encamped all around, keeping me from falling down.

Angels all around going up and down, making sure that God's word can be found.

Angels, what a wonderful gift. God has charged them to stay in our midst.

So, angels, if you didn't know, I want to tell you that I love you so.

You have done such a wonderful job, always standing guard, making sure my life is in line with the will of the Lord.

So, just let me take this time to say thank you, angels, and may God continue to bless you all in a mighty way.

I Just Need You

If I had no material things, like no car no house nor diamond ring,

It wouldn't really mean a thing, just as long as you are still King.

If I didn't have clothes, shoes or anything to eat, it would only bring me closer to your feet.

If no one spoke a word, even that would be okay, just as long as your love is here to stay, because there's nothing more important than you being here with me.

Out of all the love I have ever known, yours is the only one that lingers on.

I often wonder how this could be, you not giving up on me,

After all I have put you through, not trusting or believing in you.

But you look past all my faults and sent your Son to pay the high cost.

He came and laid down His sinless life, and throughout all history, there will never be a greater sacrifice.

So, all I need is you because you have proven to be faithful and true.

Lord, I Need a Word

Oh
Lord, I need a word from you, just one word will do.
I need to hear what you have to say. I need to hear how to make it in this world today.

Dear Lord, speak a word over my life and teach me how to serve you and live a righteous life,

How to share and care for others, how to be a good Christian sister or brother.

Sweet Lord, talk with me and say just what your plans are for me.

My Lord, I need a word in the day. I need a word when I pray. I need a word in the night through a dream for some spiritual insight.

I'll need a word all my life. I need your word to live a righteous life.

Don't Complain

I could complain about my life, how things never seem to be going right,

How the bills are always due, how I wish my boss had a clue.

I could complain about what others do, like backbiting, lying and cheating, too.

I could complain about how life's not fair, how every time I try to do right, tribulations are always there.

But I won't complain because this one thing I know is true: no matter what is going on, God will see me through.

Lord, You Always Come Through

When my mother and father can't do what I need them to do, Lord, you always come through.

When my sisters and brothers turn and walk away,
Lord, you are here and there making a way.

When my son and daughter let me down,
Here and there you are taking me to higher ground.

When friends are nowhere to be found, Lord, you are always around.

Because, Lord, you always come through, for no one loves me like you do.

I Praise

When I open my eyes to a brand new day, I know I must praise.

When I open my mouth and speak a word, I must praise. When my mind is sure of what day it is, I give God praise.

When I move one foot in front of the other, I praise. When I walk inside the house that God gave to me, I praise.

When I open the cabinet and there is food for me to eat, I praise.

When I think of the loving family that God has given to me, I praise.

I'll praise God for all these wonderful gifts, to thank Him for His mercy and faithfulness.

This is why I praise.

I Must Confess

It was one of those days when I had to press just to give praise, knowing that's not the way that it should be.

But it was one of those days when I just wasn't me.

Full of anger and some doubt, it was one of those days where I had to think myself happy if I was going to make it out.

And as the tears rolled down my face, I thought it would be a shame to lose hope and faith,

But I know it's that old enemy again trying his best to make me sin,

Standing in the background whispering lies and deceit. But he had to forgotten that it's the word of God that I listen for.

And as I press to get down on my knees, I can feel the Lord,

Strengthening me, and just as I begin to pray, my mind and heart can feel God making a way.
He has spoken a word into my soul. I'm able now to be bold,

I take a stand in all this mess and speak the word of God and confess,

I am more than a conqueror, and God hasn't lost a battle yet.

Have You Ever?

Have you ever felt like no matter what you do, it's not enough to bring you through?

You try to give your very best, but nevertheless, it's only you that's left to deal with this mess.

It feels like your prayers are bouncing off the wall. Can God really hear you at all?

Have you ever felt like your world is closing in and it's hard to determine what you need to do to make this madness end?

In spite of everything you know, it's hard to encourage yourself when you are feeling so low.
Have you ever wanted to just give in after fighting the same battle time and time again?

Well, I have come to give you hope;; don't give up now, for the blessing from your past will show you how to beat the odds for now.

Just think back on what God has already done.

That should be enough to let you know that you have already won.

For every challenge in your life, God has granted you divine and holy advice,

So whenever you start to feel low, think back on how God has already blessed you so.

I Know I'm Blessed

I woke up this morning and got on my knees to pray.
I needed to thank God for keeping me another day.

And just as I got off my knees from prayer, the devil got busy on my trail, trying to make me give up and fail.

And it was just then that I knew how powerful my prayers had to have been. Why else would the enemy be attacking me on every end?

For the enemy will stop at nothing to cause me heartache and pain.

He started confusion in my home, had my children, sister, brothers and friends fighting, even though they knew it was wrong.

He even tried killing my dog, too. I knew then that it was up to me to keep the faith and to run in this race.
With my head looking toward the sky, knowing my God still sits on high.

I'm being attacked again and again, but I know with God's power, I can win. And right then, I could feel the presence of the Lord coming and putting everything back into place, making a way for me and my family to escape.

What a joy this has been, watching my Father work it out in the end.

Weeping for a Night

Weeping may endure for a night, but we have the hope of Christ.

Weeping helps us to grow strong; with every tear drop, a new rhythm for life is born.

Weeping clears the pores; it also helps to make a way for the opening of brand new doors.

While weeping, you can't really see, but God's vision is never blurry. He sees perfectly.

Weeping, I must confess, brings great pain into my heart and chest, but when the tears have all gone away, God is there saying, "Don't you worry or get upset."

He said, "I am God, God alone. I am the power and strength you must lean on. In my word, there is truth and life; my son paid the highest price.

So weep on, my child. It's alright, for I've already made perfect the plans for your life."

In a Little While

In a little while – it won't be long – you won't even remember what went wrong.

Because the blessings of God will be so strong, you will thank God for all that went wrong.

In a little while – it won't be long – you will be singing a different song. The clouds will have gone away, and the sun will be out shining on a brand new day.

In a little while – just you wait and see – God is going to bless you and me.

Yes, in a little while – it won't be long – just keep the faith and be strong, for in a little while, God's going to right all that was wronged.

Rest a Bit

Come on in, dear, and have a seat;; it's time that you lay back and retreat. It's been a long and hard day, and you need now to relax and pray.

Lay back and close your eyes and think; start thanking God for giving you life and making the things that are wrong turn out right.

Was it something that you have done? Or, is it because of God's darling son?

Think about how far you have come, once lost in a world of sin thinking you had real friends. But just one word from the Lord, and He revealed what's in the heart.

And now that you know how much God loves you so, How would you have ever made it in this life without God's wonderful advice?

So, it's time to just rest a bit and pray that God never lets you forget about the peace that one gets when they trust in God and have a relationship.

Lord, What I Want to Be

Lord, what I want to be is a vessel worthy of serving thee.

Lord, it is important to me that I am the best that I can be.

Lord, I want to see all the things that you have planned for me.

Lord, I want to praise thee in truth and honesty.

Lord, I want you to help me take hold of my destiny.

Lord, I want you to teach me all about what love is supposed to be.

Lord, most of all, I want you to be proud of me.

You're Amazing

Dear God, you are amazing to me, the way you love so freely.

It's amazing the way you give of yourself so easily, how you bless someone like me.

Lord, it's amazing to me how you look past all my faults and tell me not to worry and have no doubts.

Dear God, you are so great to me, the only one who can judge perfectly.

Truly, you are the one and only God, you see. You are the one who created the heavens and the earth for your people to be in a place full of love, mercy and grace, in a place where your presence fills the space.

Yes, God, you are amazing to me, and you deserve worship, praise, honor and all my loyalty.

Come, Holy Spirit

Holy Spirit, come and comfort me; let me rest in only thee.

Holy Spirit, come and teach me; help me to be the woman or man that God has called me to be.

Holy Spirit, come pray with me; I need you to speak on those things I will never be able to see.

Holy Spirit, come go with me and protect me from the powers that be.

Holy Spirit, guide me; take me only to those places where I'm supposed to be.

Holy Spirit, please mold me so I can serve God as a holy vessel, the way God meant it to be, and after you have done all of that, I, too, can be holy and have a great impact on souls who don't know the real facts about how God so loved this world and what comes with that.

Holy Spirit, how I need thee; your precious spirit must cover me.

Holy Spirit, in your presence I can see all the things that God wants for me.

So, Holy Spirit, rain down on me; let the glory of your presence comfort me.

Let's Worship

Let's worship the Lord;; let's praise His holy name.
Let's make a joyful noise, one that not even the angels can sing.

Worship Him, yes, give Him the highest praise; oh, magnify, glorify and honor His holy name.

He is the beginning and the end, the first, the last, the great 'I am.'

So, worship Him in all that you do, when at work or at school,
For worship is what we were born to do.

Let us worship the Lord with a heart that is pure and true.

God Won't Forsake You

What do you do when you wake up feeling like the weight of the world is sitting on top of you?

It feels like the joy of the Lord has gone and the hope of making it through another day is slowly fading away.

You know you're doing the best that you can to live your life as a godly woman or man, but no matter what you have done, praying and calling on God in the name of the Son,

You can't see or feel victory in this present storm.

The wind has gone out of your sail;; you've said, "Oh, what the hell."

Well, here's a word just for you: just keep on praising your way through.

Don't you every give up on the Lord;; trust and believe in Him with all your heart. Out of all the things that you have been through, the one thing that you can say is that God has never forsaken you.

It's All Right

I've been up, and I've been down. I've stopped dead in my tracks

Only to find me, myself and I standing, looking all around,

Wondering, "Where did everybody go? I thought they loved me so."

Well, I've seen them come, and I've seen them go. I've heard them lie about how they loved God so.
Nevertheless, this one thing stands true. God Himself is able to bring me through, for He is the King of Kings, the Father and Creator of all things.

No matter whether I'm up or whether I'm down, God's divine glory is always around. The presence of His spirit is in my midst,
Holding me, carrying me, teaching me in times like this, showing me that He is what is known as a specialist.

Specializing in every need, be it a heartache or disease, I tell you

You just need to believe that God is all you will ever need.

A Soul's Story

Tell the story of the soul, the one that nobody knows.

No one knows the pain that lies within the soul, that very pain that got you here, that pain that keeps you near.

Near the cross of the Lord near the sound of God's beating heart,

Tell the story of the soul, of how you became bold. It wasn't because you always had the strength; it was because of God's love and tenderness.

No one knows how many nights you have cried or how many times you had to swallow your pride.

No one knows about the wee hours that you spent praying for God's help and forgiveness.

No one knows how many times you just wanted to walk away, but the ministering angels of the Lord started whispering a message to you from the Lord into your heart for that day.

Tell the story of the soul, of how the world can be so cold,
Of how by just trying to do what's right, you are engaged in a different kind of fight,

One that's of the spirit, you see, one that's not always easy to see, but you must tell the story of the soul, of how God has taken complete control,

Of how His blood came in and washed away all your sins,

Of how your life is anew and how God has brought you through,

Of how you walk in hope and faith, of how God never makes a mistake.

Just you telling the story of the soul will help someone else live a life of trying to reach God's plans and goals.

This will be written in the book of life, of how you blessed someone else's life by making such the sacrifice.

Rhythm of Life

In the rhythm of life, there are sounds that are heard in the day as well as the night, sounds of joy and sounds of pain, the sound of loved ones coming and going.

Each sound has a rhythm just the same, but these sounds are there to guide you in all that you do.

The rhythm of life makes all kind of wonderful sounds.

Sometimes, it seems like the angels in heaven are singing all around with the gentle movement of their wings that makes a melody that only the heavenly can sing.
The rhythm of life is like the harp with each string that is strummed.

A different sound of life is released, sounds of weakness, a sound of strength, a sound of confidence, a sound of shame, a sound of sweet peace when calling on Jesus' name.

And out of all the rhythms in the world, to be blessed with the rhythm of life is more precious than the finest diamonds, rubies or pearls, for you see, Jesus came into the world to give life, the rhythm, to save a dying world.

I See God

With each passing day, I can see God clearly in so many ways.

When I open my eyes, there's that joy of being alive.

When taking that first step, I know I'm being blessed.

When I look up into the sky, I can see the spirit of the Lord standing by.

He is the air that I breathe; He is in the blowing of the leaves.

He's the smell of the flowers that's all around;; He's in that shadow that you see on the ground.

He's taller than the tallest of trees;; He's in the mountains and flows through every ocean and sea.

Yes, it's easy for me to see God in everything that is surrounding me He's like a symphony inside my soul, directing me, making sure I reach His goals.

Here I Sit

Here I sit in this place filled with hurt and heartache
With no one to talk to and nowhere to escape.

Here I sit trapped in my own mind, trying to find a way to sustain.

I'm so tired of all this pain;; I'm using everything that I know, praying fasting, believing, trusting and not letting go.

But still I sit without a clue, trying my best to press through.

There are so many things that I have learned while walking with the Lord, but that doesn't stop me from trying to avoid some of the trials that must take place if I am to run this race.

But what good is it to you when you can't get past going through,

Caught up in your own web of deception, thinking things over and over in your mind, yet forgetting to call on the Lord at all times?

But I promise to look up and not look back, trusting in God, and that's a fact.

Although I don't always understand, I know God has a purpose and a plan.

He is a God that cannot lie, and on His word you can rely.

So, I'll sit here in this place for just a bit, then I'll move on in God's strength with the power and the will to live, love and forget,

Walking by faith and not by sight, trusting in the Lord with all my might.

He's a Keeper

In all the days that I have lived, God has kept me, even when I was out of His will.

He's been my father and my friend;; He's kept His word on every end.

He's been so very good to me, even when I could not see. I don't know what I would do without His mercy and grace

Keeping me through all these things, reminding me that He is the King of Kings.

Now, I have the opportunity to confess my sins, repent and pray.

So, Lord, please don't let me take for granted this brand new day that you have allow to come my way, but I'll thank you, God, forever and always for keeping me in all your ways.

Open Eyes

Lord, open my eyes that I may see just what your will is for me.

Teach me how to be strong; help me, Lord, to hold on. I want to walk in your way; I want the people to say that I am a child of the Lord and that I have a kind and giving heart

I understand now just what it means to trust in the Lord with all thy heart to allow you, Lord, to be in charge. It is when you open my eyes that I will be able to truly see what your plans are for me.

Oh, open my eyes so I can see in the way it is supposed to be, living in love and harmony, worshiping and praising God completely.

For you are God all by yourself, and we will always need your help.

Let Go and Let God

I've heard it said time and time again: let go and just leave it with Him.

But the bills are due. There's not nearly enough money to do what you need to do, but you've got to let go and let God multiply a blessing just for you.

I know your heart is heavy and your life is a mess;; it's time to let go and let God

Become your counselor and relieve you of all your stress.

Your children have gotten out of control, and you know it's that damn devil in hell after their souls. But you've got to let go and let God, for He's the one who is in control.

Now you give this advice all the time, but you seem not to pay it any mind. How could this be?
How could it be good for all others, but you have yet to discover to let go and let God, for if you truly believe that He is like no other, you must let go and let God.

If you are to recover from what's been broken, you must trust God, even when words have not been spoken.

So, just let go and let God, for He's more than able to take care of you.

A Talk with the Lord

I had a talk with the Lord. I began to tell Him just what was in my heart. Although, He really didn't need to hear what I had to say because He reads my heart every day, but nevertheless, He lets me say whatever I thought I needed to say anyway.

I began telling Him just how I felt about waiting on His promises to be revealed. I told Him about how I get upset and how I start thinking that they may not manifest.

I talked about how sometimes, I wonder why those who don't even know Him seem to be getting more than just getting by;; they've got theirs and my supply. It seems like all their needs are being met, and they never even think about giving Him any respect.

Yet, they go on living their dreams and romancing the world and all its things while the saints of God are standing by looking and wondering when, where and why.

But then, I think about your sweet mercy and grace and when the day comes when we meet face to face. I then understand why you call me the apple of your eye, for your plans for me are much higher than I could ever really know or understand. For each and every day you just keep on blessing me.

There's no end to your love;; you proved that by shedding your precious blood. So, thank you for having this talk with me, for you are more than just my Holy Father, you see; you are a best friend to me.

The Goodness of the Lord

When I think about the goodness of the Lord, my heart leaps for joy. When I think about all He has done, it gives me the power to overcome. When I think about the gift of His son, there are no words that can explain why I sing and shout at the very mention of His holy name.

When I think about the goodness of the Lord, I wonder why it took me so long to find my way into His loving arms because life has never been so sweet, and I feel so complete. Yes, I wasted a lot of time, but God said, "Pay that no mind. Come now and began to live your life with an expected end, expecting to see my face in the end, knowing I am God, your father and friend. I ordain your expected end."

So, let's just think about the goodness of the Lord and never depart out of the presence of His sight by praising Him with all our might.

God's Favor

The favor of the Lord will always be better than that of man, for it is God who holds all power in the palms of His hands.

God's favor is not like that of man. You won't have to worry about what kind of mood He's in, for His grace and mercy will never end.

The favor of God is better than that of man. He will be fair and just; on this you can depend.

The favor of God will stand the test of time. Just ask the patriarchs of old Abraham, Isaac, even Job.

The covenant and promises that He made still blesses us, even to this day.

Yes, the favor of God is better than that of man. Just believe, trust and worship Him so he can lead you to your divine end.

To Be Used by God

What a wonderful thing, to be used by God,

To be the one in whom He can trust to care for the souls that don't know Him yet,

To be that one who will stand and move only at His command,

To tell someone about God's plan, the one to save all men,

To be the hands that would touch and heal, to be the feet that would walk up and down ungodly streets and hills, professing that it is God that the world must meet in order to live and have true love and peace.

Yes, it's a wonderful thing to be used by God, to be His hands and His feet, to be His holy mouthpiece, to speak of life and love and tell of heaven above.

Not Just Another Day

Today is a great day! Will you take the time to pray?

Pray not only for yourself, but take some time to pray for someone else.

Let's take time this day to invite God in and allow Him to be our father and best friend.

I'll take this day to help someone along the way, and when they are feeling all by themselves, I'll tell them to call on God. He'll give them help.

Just take this day and begin to think about God's goodness and grace, about how His love never ends. He's always there;; on that you can depend.

And when you have done all these things, I guarantee the joy it will bring. It's not just another day when you know what the word of God has to say.

It's the Season

Well, it's that time of the year when everyone is making plans for celebration and cheer.

This is the season to care and share, to give and to receive, to be more understanding and thoughtful of others' needs.

But all doesn't feel this way. To them, it's a time of 'oh, no' and 'make this pain please go away.'

It's hard to understand why the holidays are good for some, while others just want to find a place to run.

Well, I guess it must be just this: we somehow have forgotten the who, what, when and how of all of it

We've forgotten just what the cost really was for us to be able to live and love and walk in the righteousness sent from above.

You see, it's much more than buying someone a pair of nice leather gloves.

It's about the shedding of innocent blood, and when we forget about the blood that was shed out of love, we lose the real meaning of the reason for the holiday season.

So, yes, it's that time of the year when we celebrate the gift of life, love and the blessings of God above.

So, when the season comes around, don't get upset and start feeling down. Just take this time to really celebrate the mercies of God and keep the faith.

My Special Valentine

There is no bigger heart than yours, one who gives and shares His love.

You never think about the cost, even when we are lost.

Your heart pumps out more than blood; it pumps out pure, divine love.

The way you do so many things earns you the right to be called the King of Kings.

You're the King of Hearts, the King of Love, the King of all that's true to love, and I just wanted you to know that you are my special Valentine and I love you so.

December Anew

On a cold December night, I lie awake in my bed wondering what's ahead.

The old year is about to end, and a new one is coming in.

What will be the challenge for me? There's always something, you see.

Will I be able to really see the plans that God has for me and how will I handle my next catastrophe?

And what will I do in my success? Will I remember to bless God and not forget of all His holy goodness?

And just what do I want this New Year to bring? It's got to be more than just tangible things.

I want more love, joy and peace and a closer walk with God beyond what I can imagine or think.

Yes, December is going out, and a new year is about to begin.

But what I want most of all is to be called God's child and friend.

Happy

Happy are those who rejoice in the Lord, for they know who gives out real rewards.

Happy are those who pray, for they have seen the hand of God each and every day.

Happy are those who give, for they will never live to see a day of lack. In fact, they will always get back.

Happy are those who care, for they bring hope to many souls that are feeling despair.

Happy are those who understand that loving, caring and sharing are gifts from above, and only God can give to someone such a heart with that kind of love.

So, happiness is just a state, but one must make something happen in order for it to take place.

Happy is what happy does, so let's make the world a happy place, by showing God's kind of love.

Entering In

I am entering into the best season in my life. Through all the trauma and trials that I have been through, I have learned to trust the love of God to see me through.

No one knows about the hurt and pain of trying to withstand.

But I'm entering into the best season in my life, and it's all because of Jesus Christ.

How many times did I believe that God had forgotten about me?

Or how many times did I get upset because I didn't think to remember and I chose to forget,

Just where God has brought me from and forgetting how the battle was won?

Yes, the best is yet to come, and the season that God promised has just begun.

I can thank God now and really mean it because it was through those trials and hard times that I could conceive just how much God really loves me.

Storm

A storm arose in the night, bringing powerful winds, lighting and fright.

We all ran for cover, you see, but who or what could really shield us from the powers that be?

We were scared of what may come after the storm, realizing that all the food was gone.

Help, they said, is on the way, but some decided this would be a good time to learn how to pray.

Could the word of the Holy Bible be true? Could it be that the God of heaven and earth is still with us, too?

When it stormed in the days of old, God sent His wrath upon all unwilling souls.

Let's not let it happen again, for the Bible said not water this time, but by fire, my friend.

Pray, Pray, Pray

Pray, come what may.

Pray to the Lord each and every day.

Pray so you and He can talk,
For God already knows your thoughts.

Pray for direction; pray for insight.

Pray for God's holy advice.

Pray for strength; pray for peace.

Pray when your heart is heavy and when you are feeling weak.

Pray, pray, pray is what we must do,
because God hears, and He will answer you.

Faith Revealed

My heart was so heavy, my spirit so weak, my soul was in turmoil, I was leaning toward defeat.

My thoughts were so low, I could not speak, and I did not understand why I had no peace.

Then, I began to see just what you have been telling me.

Lean not toward your own understanding, and trust in me.

Put faith in nothing or no man, just believe that I am.

Know that I am God and God alone, and if you stay with me, you will never go wrong.

Under the Sky

Under the dark, blue sky, the stars are shining as the rain drops from above. You have to know it's just God showing His love.

Although I'm a long way from home, because God loves me, I'm never alone.

His mercies are new each and every day, and that's why I love to pray.

I want to thank Him for His grace, His compassion and for Him giving me faith.

It's because of His love in my life that I'm able to do what's right.

No more living recklessly, letting sin take over me, but I'll live free knowing the blood of Jesus covers me.

Yes, as I sit under the dark sky, I can see now that I am the apple of God's eye.

Satan Can't Stop My Praise

Satan, you can't stop my praise. You didn't give it to me, and you can't take it away.

Satan, you have no power over me, so take your imps and get away from me.

Satan, you are such the fool, thinking the tactics that you use will cause me to lose, but instead, I get down on my knees to thank my God for saving me.

Satan, you're the one who is a defeated foe, and you know God has already blessed my soul. So, Satan, get out of my way;; I don't have time to play. You know to play all those silly little games, the ones where you are trying to make me sin and disgrace my God's holy name.

Me glorifying my God's name, Satan, that won't ever change because He is greater than any stress or strain that you may try to proclaim.

But I will praise and worship Him, for He has been better than good to me, and He deserves the very best of me.

So, Satan, you can't stop my praise. You didn't give it to me, and you can't take it away.

An Unfamiliar Place

I'm in this unfamiliar place trying to find some space.

I don't really know how I got to this state;; I know I need to find a way of escape. Things seem to be going all wrong;; sometimes I don't want to leave my home.

What can I do to change the pace? I must stop and contemplate to view or consider this unfamiliar place.

What did I do to get in this state? Have I stopped being considerate of others feelings and faith?

Have I become too involved with my own state? I can't seem to focus on my own mistakes. Have I not put enough time into praying, or have I decided to wait till the next day? Have I lost control of my flesh, and has it stopped me from getting much-needed rest?

Could it be that I'm not in the wrong, and it's just time to grow and be strong? Whatever the case may be, I know that it's hard for me, but I know without a doubt the God I serve will bring me out.

Somewhere

Somewhere across this land, someone has lost a loved one and friend and now is left feeling nothing but hurt and despair,

Scared to even think about them not being there.

They're finding it hard to understand why God called them now; this couldn't have been His plan.

The impact of losing them can't be explained, missing the way that they talked, smiled and called your name,

Wondering and asking, "Lord, why and how could this be,

Knowing, Lord, just how much they meant to me?

Yet, even in this pain, I find it strange that I can have peace just by calling Jesus' name.

Then, I'm reminded of the fact that God knows about such pain, you see; He experienced it first when Jesus Christ was slain. And although someone that you loved is gone, let me encourage you to hold on because just as God has always been there,

He will never leave you because He truly cares.

So, keep your eyes on the Lord, pray and keep Him close to your heart, for no matter what you are going through, God will be with you.

In the memory of the mothers who lost their children

On 7/9/06 in the Meramec River, may God continue to keep and bless you.

Our Mother and Friend

Only God knew how to pick someone like you to be our mother and our friend, someone who would love us through thick and thin.

He placed you in our lives because He knew you would be willing to do what you had to in order to make us strong; we know now that it was God that you learned to lean on.

What a great woman of love! God had to send you from above, with such style and grace, knowing whose you are while running this race, the daughter of the most high God, our mother and our friend, our blessing to the end.

They're Gone

To lose someone that you love is hard to bear, but even through those times, you must still believe that God is there.

The pain and the devastation of losing that loved one has a way of lingering on. Was there something more you could have done that would have made a difference in their life?

Now is truly the time to believe that God knows and is in control of all your needs.

Cry as you may, and let the pain be washed away. They tell me tears are just liquid prayers that God has bottled up because He cares.

Remember, trouble won't last for long, and you are not in this all alone. God promised that He would be there, so you don't have to lose any sleep;; just rest in God's peace.

But the pain of the loss is so strong, and the thought of not seeing that loved one hurts you down to the bone.

What can you do to end all this hurt? Just trust in God and watch Him work.

Sunshine

The sun will shine for you and for me.
There won't always be this dark cloud following you or me,

For our hope is in the Lord, you see, and we can't believe in everything that we see.

And although things don't look good, we'll just keep our eyes upon the Lord like we should.

For we know without a shadow of a doubt that it is our God who makes the sun come out, so when the sun is hard to see, just remember the son of God whose love shines farther than the eye can see.

Fifty

What a blessing to be fifty years old! We praise God for watching after your soul. We know life has not always been good at fifty years; there are times when you must have been misunderstood.

But through it all, you have not been alone, for the God of heaven and earth has given you the strength to go on.

At fifty years old, you have surely seen some things.

You've seen what a mother's love can do;; you've felt what it was like to have your father stand by you.

You have watched your sisters and brothers grow;; you've
even been a blessing to their souls. You've had friends come and go; you have prayed for God to bless their souls.

There have been doors to open and to close, and that's how you learn to let God be in control. Fifty years old, what a wonderful gift.

It's a present from God to allow you to exist.

So may you have fifty more years to come, and with each year to come, may you resemble God's holy son.

Uncommon Favor

Uncommon favor is in my life;; that's why it looks like I'm not in a fight.

It's that favor from God up above;; it comes with walking in God's perfect love.

Uncommon favor most don't understand;; they think it has something to do with man.

But man has nothing to do with this. Trust me;; it's just God's goodness.

Uncommon favor does not fall on all;; it's for that special soul, the one who allows God to be in complete control.

It's knowing that God has called you out from the rest and given you the best of the best.

You walk in peace, love and victory, praising God for such wonderful liberties. It's God's uncommon favor that's upon me.

I am the redeemed of the Lord. I walk by faith and not by sight. I have the power of dominion over my life. God spoke it, and I know it's true. Look at me;; you see it, too.

Yet, you don't quite understand. You think it has something to do with man.

You know man can't give this. This comes from God above, uncommon favor and unconditional love.

PIECE TWO

Just My Thoughts

CONCERN, CONSIDERATION, THE GOOD LORD IS OUR CONSTANT HELP

Just My Thoughts

Look at Me	56
Praise the Lord	57
Joy	58
A Letter to God	59
What Then?	60
Fight	61
While Standing	62
What Can I Say?	63
The New Year	64
This Girl	65
Didn't You Know?	66
How Can I?	67
God is Real	68
God, it Had to be You	69
Mom and Dad	70
It's Not About Me	71
Feelings	72
Where Would I Be?	73
Lonely	74
Bridesmaid	75
I Can't Sleep	76
Peace	77
Addiction	77
God Loves You	79
Sick	80
Faith	81
Humiliation	81
Walking	82
I Love the Lord	82
Passed Away	83

Gone Home	84
Remember	85
So You Thought	85
The Goodness of the Lord	86
No Greater Love	87
It's My Time	88
Expectation	89
Good Morning	89
Turning the Corner	90
Sometimes	90
You Can Win	91
Choose	92
You Are Special	92
Hope	93

Look at Me

Look at me now.
I am not the same as before.
A change has taken place.
Maybe I can explain.

I found out that I am the child of the highest God,
That I am wonderfully, marvelously made and when I
was born, the angels in heaven celebrated my birth and
called my name.

Look at me now.
I don't walk the same.
I don't even talk the same .
There has been a great change .

I walk with my head held up high.
I pay attention to the things that I pass by.
I talk with great pride.
I have confidence in the things that I feel inside.
I know who I am and why I am alive.

Look at me now.
I don't think the way that I used to,

And my feelings have changed about many things.

My hope is not in me.
It is in the God of the whole universe.

And what a relief. I can hardly believe that life is so easy
for me.

Look at me now.
I can live life in the way God planned for me,

Not worrying about how I am going to make it

From one day to the next.
God has already promised to take care of that.

Look at me now.
I am blessed.
I have no regrets.
I thank God for the many tests.

They are making me stronger,
And I have so much to confess
About the love of God and His goodness.

Look at me now.
I have joy.
I have peace.
I have love enough to want to seek life
In a very different way,

In away to help others in making their day.

Praise the Lord

I will praise you, Lord, everyday,
For this is what I was born to do,
And I am so glad that you chose me, too.

When the things of this world seem to bring me down,
I lift my eyes up to the sky and see your presence standing by.

Quickly, I am reminded just then
that I was born to win.

And everything that was set up to hold me back and make me feel as if I was trapped

Has to come in line with the fact that I am the head, and in God, there is no lack.

Let's not forget about the pain, and strain of knowing
that there's a need for great change.

The bills are due,
and the rent is late, too.
What will you do?

This will be the time to tap into your faith, for God will
make away for your escape.

Yes, I will praise the Lord with all my heart,

For He has loved me from the start.
He gave up His only son just so you and I could be one,

One with God, you see,
and join Jesus to help set the captive free.

Joy

Joy is letting the word of God penetrate deep within
your soul.

Joy is sweet peace, and great relief.

Joy is something that exists in the storm.
It never seems to loose it's form.

Joy is that smile that most do not understand ,

How can you smile with all the trouble that you are in?

It's because joy comes from God and not from men.

The joy God gives you belongs to you,
And no one can take it away but you.

Joy does not come to everyone.
It only comes to those who seek God's son,

For He has made the ultimate sacrifice, by laying down His life.

Now joy belongs to Him, you see,
And He wants you to have it because it is free.

A Letter to God

I thank you, God, for the gift of life.
You have made such a difference in my life.

It is like tasting spice.
Sometime it's bitter.
Sometime it's sweet,
but mixed with the right ingredient, it's always a treat.

I truly want to give you praise.
I want to bless your holy name.

I know for myself why all heaven and earth should proclaim,

Just how great you are,
And sing praises to your name.

You are the one and only King.
Your name shall always ring supreme.

I don't want to ever stop lifting up your name.

I want to thank you, and thank you, and thank you again. I don't want my thank you's to ever end.

For you are my father, my lover and best friend,
and you have proven it time and time again.

What Then?

What then,
When the very reason you started has now become the reason why you want it to end?

What then,
When your life seems to make no sense? Could you have wasted too much time on foolishness?

What then,
When you have planned this thing for the last seven years of your life, only to find out that you might not have gotten it right?

What then,
When you have lost your best friend, and you feel like this is the end?

What then,
When you have no choice but to walk out God's ordained plan for your life?

There is no time to complain.
This life sentence will not change
Simply because it has been ordained.

What then,
When you do not know whether to go out or stay in, and you cannot explain what you feel? Does that make it less real?

What then,
When things need to start, stop, and begin? The choices that you make will determine whether you will win in the end.

These what's and then's have always been, and on top of that, they were set up to trap you in.

But the good news about all of this is that God has already taken care of the "what,"

And the "then" belongs to Him.

And He provided the "when" to be your friend in the end.

Fight

When going through strife in your life, how do you stay in control of the fight?

By looking at the light of the world.
His name is Jesus Christ.

You must know your position and pay close attention.
You must have strong resistance.

I should make mention that there is more then one reason why you must fight.
It has to do with the things of life.

Although the clouds are gray, God has set up a brighter day.

When you feel like all your strength has gone,
God will be there for you to lean on.

Stand up and fight, for God gave you this right,

And the devil has no power over you.
God would not have said it if it wasn't true.

Fight in spite of all your circumstances.

This will be the way of great advances.

You will have to pull down strongholds.
This power comes from within your soul.

All of heaven is on your side.
The word will be your guide,
weapon and your shield.

It will cut through any problems every revealed.

You must fight in the day as well as the night,

But keep your head up and never give up,
Continue to fight with all your might, for God said
everything is all right.

While Standing

While I was standing in the wings of my new beginnings,
a few things began to take place.

I first had to look at my surrounding space.
I had to figure out what needed to stay or what had to
go.

While standing, things became very uncomfortable
sometimes.
I wanted to leave this place,
But my faith said no, you are in the right space.

While standing, my heart would break,
But I knew I just needed to wait
And the mending would soon take place.

While standing, I learn that it was not about the race,
But who will be left standing in place.

While standing, my knees would sometime buckle,
And at that time, I knew it was much deeper than just the struggle.

While standing, the tears would sometimes flow,
But by morning, I wondered, where did they go?

While standing, laughter sometime came hard,
But because I knew the Lord, He put joy back into my heart.

While standing, I knew I was set apart.
I knew I had favor from the Lord,
And it is He who has kept me standing through it all.

What Can I Say?

What can I say?
I never knew it would be this way.
This thing changes from day to day.

What can I say?
It is all new to me. I fight a spiritual battle constantly.
I am so glad that my hope is not in me.
If that were the case, I would not be.
No, not me.

But I am learning daily not to let my thoughts control me, but to let the spirit of the Lord console me.

I often wonder why things would happen to me.
Is it because I have an ordained destiny, and the dark spirit of this world is trying to stop me?

Yes! That is what it must be,
But I can't let it. No! I've got to make it so that all the world can see

That living for God is the best choice out of all the
choices, you see.

What can I say?
I guess I can say a lot of things.
I can say even though it has not always been fun,
I have been assured the battle has already been won.

I could say that after the storm,
the sun always performs.

I could say that through the many tears and pain, the joy
of the Lord remains.

What can I say?
I can truly say that God is the one and only way,

And if you invite Him into your heart to stay, there are
no boundaries when God is leading the way.

The New Year

Today starts the beginning of a new year.
God has chosen to keep me here.

I need to remember what I learned last year
so I will not repeat the same disappointments for this
year.

This year will be even greater for me, you see.
I have grown in the Lord tremendously.

I learned last year how to confess the things of God with
great pride and boldness,
For God has given me His confidence.

I also learned that it was up to me to choose what I
wanted this year to be

By working towards my goals in life, and making sure I get the best advice.

This advice can only come from Jesus Christ, for he is the only one with perfect insight.

It is the start of a brand new year.
My plan is for God to always be near.
By doing this, I won't have to fear, for I'll rest in Gods confidence all year.

This Girl

Once upon a time, there was a girl.
She lived life for the world.

She never knew what she was born to do,
so most of her dreams never came true.

She tried to do things this way and tried to do them that way,
But all the things she tried never seemed to turn out to be the right way.

She soon picked up a book.
She did not just look,
But she read what was in this book.

This book was not like any other.
It told about the meaning of love, life
and how to live forever.

She now knew what she needed to do
in order to live life and to have faith that was true.

She had a new heart, and now she would be able to serve the Lord.

She could now be true to love,
True to life, true to the things that would make a difference in someone else's life.

Who is this girl?

Well, it's me.

Didn't You Know?

Didn't you know that God loves you so? He sent his son so that you and I could be one.

He gave the angels charge to stand guard all around you Because He wants the world to know that you have Him deep within your soul.

It is a wonderful thing, knowing that your daddy is the King of Kings,
And He has given you authority over all earthly things.

Didn't you know you were born to be bold and to command and demand what is right in your soul.

Didn't you know that the earth belongs to the Lord and the fullness thereof,
and He has allowed you to be the steward of
all these things? What a joy this should bring.

Didn't you know that the love of God is a known fact, and no matter what, He will never take His love back?
Didn't you know that?

How Can I?

How can I expect things to change when I keep doing the same old thing?

I only have myself to blame.

I feel so ashamed.

How can I go forward when I am constantly looking backwards,

Thinking that my past will change? I know this is strange.

How can I love you when I have yet learn to love myself?

It's impossible. I must confess, this will untimely turn into a mess.

How can I blame you for my life's disappointments when it has always been me who accepted your grand performances?

How can I expect something from you that I am not willing to do?

That's not the way it should be.

Please, forgive me.

How can I go on with my life in spite of all the disappointment, grief and strife?

By praising God with all my might, for it was He who gave me life.

God is Real

How do you know that God is real?

When looking at the sky, what does that reveal?

When you see the stars way up high or watch the clouds as they float by,

Who placed the sun and moon in the sky?

When looking at all these things, does it not reveal that God is real?

When looking at the movement from the breeze, stirring up the leaves on the trees,

This is just their way of praising God, you see.

When you feel the air on your skin
from the chill of the wind, what then?

Perhaps you thought about a man. I tell you, you must think again

Because without God, there is no man, and man never really had a plan.

He was just the result of some dirt

That God decided was worth blowing into

Because it was God's divine plan
that we should all say, "Amen."

God, it Had to be You

God, it had to be you who kept me through it all. So many times after all my many falls, you allow me to stand tall.

I know it was you that called me out of darkness into the light. Who else cared about my life?

It had to have been you to make me want to live again
When so many times I just wanted it all to end,
But you kept on being my best friend.

God, it had to have been you

Who changed my heart when at times, I would act as if I never knew the Lord.

God, it had to be you

Who taught me how to turn and walk away
When other wise, I would have stayed.
I didn't even have enough sense to be afraid.

Yes, you told me to focus on you
and to try to do as you, and learn how to forgive others the way that you do,

To love them in away that is true, not fake or phony, but in away that will bless them only.

God, only you could teach someone like me to be the best that I can be.

In such a unique and wonderful way, you put your mark on me to stay.

God, my life will never be the same.

That's why I sing you praises and lift up your Holy name.

So, I hope someone can see that there is a God just by looking at me.

Mom and Dad

This poem is for my dad and mom, for they are reason why I am around.

I thank God for parents like you two because you loved and trusted God to see you through.

Then, you took the time to teach your children, too, That God was the only one that could see us through.

And because of this marvelous deed, we are able to live our lives so differently.

We know not to put our trust in man, But to keep holding on to Jesus' hand

Because God has already paid the price, and this has given us the choice to taste the spice of life.

So, I thank you for letting God be the head of your lives, for this is what is known as true wisdom for life.

Truly, I am blessed to have the both of you, and I want to take this time and say thank you.

Love,
Teresa

It's Not About Me

It's not about me. It's about the God in me.

I never would have known that He existed if I had never come upon some disappointments.

That is when I had to turn and look within, and I found out that it was more to me than just flesh and skin.

There was this force of life that I had not yet tapped into.

This thing was much more powerful than I can explain. It started me to make a great change.

I learned that I needed to go down in order to elevate.

I had to have pain in order to learn how to restrain.

I would have to have many sleepless nights in order to learn how to fight.

There were lots of tears before I could control my fears because it was not about me.

So, God let me know why He trusted me so.

He knew He owns my body and soul, but He allows me to take the time to learn how to stay in control.

There will be no place for foolish pride, doubts or lies

Because it is not about me, but God, you see.

Feelings

Why do I feel the way that I feel? Sometimes it's hard to deal with these feelings that I feel.

There are times when I feel like my heart has been healed, and then out of nowhere the cracks are revealed.

There have been times when I feel this great love all around, and then all of a sudden it's nowhere to be found.

Sometimes I feel like I can take the whole world on, and in just one moment, the feeling is gone.

There are times that I feel close to my sisters, my brothers, my parents, and my friends; then there are times when I feel like they don't know me and I don't know them.

I know that some feelings can change, and There are others that will remain the same.
Nevertheless, they are apart of our life's conquest.

Sometimes these feelings can lead us right, and other times they can turn our days into midnight.

These feelings can be a mighty force.
They will dictate a person's choice.

That is why you need to know it is your job to keep your feelings in control,

For if you don't, you see,
you will leave this easily moved emotion to give you the notion to dictate your devotion.

You see, feelings are strange and sometimes hard to explain,

But it doesn't change the fact that our feelings carry with them great impact.

So, take care of your feelings
the best that you can,
and after you have done that,

Give God control over all the feelings that you lack.

Where Would I Be?

If it had not been for the Lord, where would I be?

I would be lost in this world, thinking that I was free.

I would still be digging myself a ditch, not knowing that I'm going to fall in it.

I would still be walking with the devil to and fro
Without a clue that he was after my soul.

I wouldn't be able to see the forest,
Just the trees, and I would not have known that all this damn drama in my life started with me.

But God, you see, was and is the key.

I have given Him my life, and He has shown me just where I am suppose to be.

Lonely

I have no one. I am all alone.
I thought about something that was funny. I had no one
to tell. That's when I remembered I was lonely.

I saw a movie the other day. There were some things I
wanted to say.
But there was no one to share, and I remembered I was
alone.

I have some decision to make, some circumstances and
situations have taken place. Who can I turn to,
To help me contemplate? And I remembered I am all
alone in this space

I made up my face, I fixed my hair,
I picked out a pretty dress to wear,
Then I looked into the mirror with great despair because
there was no one to care, and I remembered I am alone

There's no children in the house anymore.
There's no need to say, "Shut the door, get off the phone,
and it's time for your friends to go home," and I
remembered I am all alone

I was invited to a party the other night. I didn't make it
because it just didn't feel right.
I mean, I didn't feel like being without
a date. It's probably best to stay at home.
I don't really want to be alone.

I got a phone call today. It was to tell me that someone
special to me had passed away.

I wanted to be held tight, to here that everything was all
right, and I remembered I was alone.

I cried myself to sleep that night,
But in my dream, I was not alone. There was a King on a throne.

He stood up with his arms open wide.
He said, "Come sit down by my side
And let me tell you what you do not see."

Although you are feeling so lonely, remember I love you strongly.

I have set you aside because you are a special bride, and I have blessed you with a different kind of pride.

You know of your self-worth. You are a queen here on earth,

And because you live your life for the Lord, I will give you a great reward.

Just remember to keep your eyes upon me, and know that you are not alone.
You are with me.

Bridesmaid

Always a bridesmaid and never the bride – did you every stop to think why?

Maybe it is because you are so special and you chose God to direct your holy vessel.

You see things different from others. You know there is more to love than just being lovers.

You know it takes a special gift to share with others, and it is a good thing to be friends before you are lovers.

You know that when a person loves the Lord, it shows through, and there is no need to put up your guards.

You won't have to protect your heart.
You know that when you say, "I do," the Lord would have given them to you.

Who else knows what's best for you?

Now because you are so special, it will take time to pursue a deserving vessel.
Yes, always a bridesmaid and never the bride, you need to thank God for setting you aside.

I Can't Sleep

I can't sleep. Something is trying to take my peace.
A lot has taken place this past week, and my emotions are at their highest peak.

You need to know this is not something new to me.
This happens when God is moving me,

Taking me to another level in Him, preparing me for life's good times as well as the struggles.

My spirit is trying to tell me something.
I need to be still and listen, making sure to pay close attention.

But it won't come until the right moment. That is when God knows I can stand on it,

Standing on His word without a doubt because I know He has already worked it out.

God has prepared my heart and mind for such a time, and I know everything is fine.

Peace

I thank God for peace of mind. I would not trade it in for a gold mine

Out of all the things in life I find, there's nothing quite like peace of mind.

Peace of mind is better than the finest of wine that has been aged from the beginning of time.

When you have peace, there is always light, even in the darkest of nights.

You can't find peace in material things like cars, houses, money or diamond rings. These things bring joy but not for long, it seems.

Some go a lifetime only having peace in a dream, and this is a sad thing.

Nevertheless, for those of you who want to know, I'll tell you this before I go: Peace is something that comes from within. It is given from God and not from men.

Addiction

Addicted is what I am;; I crave for things that most don't understand.
Some would like to believe that I am just weak and I am living my life in defeat.

I try. I try with all my might,
But it seems like am loosing this fight.
I do things that I don't want to.
I take things from others; yes, it's true.

But you need to understand that it's not in my plan. I am addicted to things that I don't understand.

I am not like most others. Without my "fix," it is hard for me to love my brothers.

Some say that it is a disease,
And well, I will have to agree
That this disease has taken control over my mind, my body and my soul.

I no longer want to live like this, waking each day, looking for my next "fix."

I am in search now for a cure.
I don't know how much longer I can endure with this pain for a "fix."

I need a drink, a snort or just one hit.
I don't want to turn another trick.

I was told that God was the key.
I need to get with Him quickly.
I need a remedy.

They tell me, God, that I am still your child. Although we have not talked in a while, I want to ask you back into my life. Please help me to get it right.

I want to take this time to say
Forgive me, Lord, and ask you back into my heart to stay.

I will confess all my sins.
I know with Jesus Christ I can win.

There is nothing left for me to say
But thank you, Lord, for making a way.

God Loves You

Just when it seems like all hope is gone, you show up
and straighten out all that was wrong.

You sit high and you look low,
Watching all your children down below.

You know that we are constantly under attack,
Trying our best to keep the devil back.

You promise to be with us at all times, and it is up to us
to keep this in mind.

No matter what the problem may be, God is more than
able to set us free.

With one word whispered out of His mouth,
He takes away any need to doubt.

He said, "Come, love, and worship me,
and I will supply all of your needs.

I am your father. Yes, it is true.
I chose to love you before you knew.

You were in my plans from the start.
You are my children, and I am your Lord.

There is nothing that can come
between us. Just believe in my word and trust.

Yes, I know all things at all times
because I keep you on my mind."

Love,
God

Sick

I just got the news today .
The doctor said I was sick and to get to the hospital right away.
They came and stood by my bedside
with this list, and they read.

They read off all these things. It was like some kind of a bad dream.
I did not know just what to do.
This thing was much more than the flu.

Right then and there, all I could feel was great despair.

Then the Lord entered in and reminded me of whom I had become after accepting His son.

He said that the power was in me, and Jesus Christ has set me free.
I have been healed by the blood, and I belong to God up above.

And no sickness or disease could every really kill me

Because absent from the body, present with the Lord, sitting in heavenly places, oh my Lord.

So, sick is not what I am.
I am just transforming to go into heavenly land.

(Dedicated to the memory of P. Frederick)

Faith

I am standing on faith, but it's not my own.

It comes from God. He is the only one I can lean on.

This substance that I must hope on gives me opportunity to grow strong.

God's faith is like no other;; the peace it gives will last forever.

When I feel like I am all alone, the faith I have in God's love makes me press on.

I know not to put trust in what I see, but I must believe in what God's word is telling me.

Without the word, there is no faith, and without faith, nothing good can really take place.

So, I will take God's word and build my faith.
By doing this, I know I will win this race.

Humiliation

(The quality or state of being humble)

I felt like I was done wrong.
I need to show you that I am strong.
I do not need anyone to lean on.
It is not important for me to hear what you have to say.
Things must go my way.

Please, forgive me, for I am wrong.
To be able to forgive others makes me strong.
I know we all need someone to lean on.

I have to learn not to take away from you, just to make my way through.
It is important for me to hear what you have to say, and things will ultimately go God's way.

Walking

I'm learning a lot in this walk.
I can't get comfortable in one spot.
In order to be what God has chosen for me to be,
I've got to be able to move freely.

I am to set a standard for others to see.
When they look at me, they should want to follow my God, not me.

They need to know that my God is the best and He is the only one who is able to bless.

I am walking, taking one step at a time, learning to stay in God's line.

I am learning a lot in this walk.
I know it's my duty to praise God and worship Him with a shout.

I Love the Lord

I love the Lord, for He has been so good to me.
He has kept His hand upon me
And did not allow me to give up on me.

He open my eyes and let me see the true meaning of life and what it is suppose to be.
He cleared my ears so that I could hear.
I heard His word, and then I knew there was an assigned job that I must do.

He touched my heart so I could feel.
Now I can love others, for this is God's will.

I love the Lord with all my heart,
For it was He who gave me a choice.
And I could chose to live for Him or
I could continue to live in sin.

Yes, I love the Lord, you see, because He first loved me.

Passed Away

Passed away…
I just got the news today that a good friend of the family
has just passed away.

It makes me wonder what to say
to the family after losing a loved one in such a way.

Words just cannot seem to say just how hurt I feel,
But the pain for the family is more than real.

Still, life will go on in a strange and unique way.
We must learn to live without that special someone with
each passing day.

Now the impact on your life that they made
Seems to stand out in an unusual way.

You never really understood that their presence in your
life was for your own good.

They helped to mold out the character that is within.
That is why God chose them to be your friend.

So, we thank God for our friends,
knowing his or her memory will live on in the end.

Because you can feel their presence all around, there is no reason to be down.

(Dedicated in the memories of
E. Putman/ S.Hudson/A. Bowers a.k.a. Niecy
H. Meyers/J.Foster/ A. Simpson
J. Miller and Joyce)

Gone Home

If you are here in this room today, it is obvious that I have passed away.

Now do not be sad or get upset because I got things straight with God before I left.

I know you will miss me and I will miss you, too, but this day was planned before I met you.

You must understand that my time is up.
I gave my life to God, and in Him you must trust.

If you could only see just how beautiful it is up here,

Then you could understand why I would choose not to leave here, my dears.
It is so much better here.

The only thing that I would ask of you
Is to seek God in all that you do.

Let Him be at the top of your list; talk with God and start a relationship.

I hope to see you again one day,

But until then, I will be here in heaven, cheering you in.

Remember

I remember a time when it seemed like every door had been shut in my face,

When I could only hope to be strong,
When it seemed like everything was going wrong,

When the facts just did not add up,
When the word of God seemed not to attack,

To attack the problems that were at hand, and I have been told to just stand,

When the enemy looked like he had won, and it felt like I was all alone,
Lord knows I didn't want to go on.

Then, I remembered just who I was,
A child of God that sits high above.

So, I told the enemy to take his place under my foot and do not make a mistake,

Because I use the word of God to determine my fate, and I will always be in first place.

So You Thought

So you thought that there were horn on my head and you thought that my eyes were red; you thought I had a tail too and all the time I look just like you.

I wake up each morning and comb my hair, I pick out the finest things to wear making sure my smile is nice and bright my plan is to take a soul without a fight.

I am that person that you just let in
that one who will ruin you in the end.
And if you let me into your heart,
I guarantee you will disobey your Lord.

My color changes all the time; I come in black, white,
and red or brown, wherever you are, I am around.

My words sound sweet, and most of the time, I can make
you cheat.

I am that young, pretty thing that you can't get out of
your dreams.

I am mister right with all my wrongs. I am the one that
will break up your home.

So you think you know who I am.
I am that one who holds up holy hands.
I can beat you saying hallelujah and amen,
And with that same tongue I'll curse you in the end
Because I look just like you my friend.

So you thought I was your friend,
And all this time I have been encouraging you to sin.
And every time you give in to your flesh, you pass my
design test.

And so you thought you knew.
I have to wonder; maybe you do.

The Goodness of the Lord

The goodness of the Lord is more than you and I will
ever know,
Because He does things behind the scenes to bless us so.

The goodness of the Lord comes in like a flood,

Making great tracks in the mud.

The goodness of the Lord is a wonderful thing,
It helps to complete those special dreams.

The goodness of the Lord is like no other; it can lift up bowed down heads and make you forgive others.

The goodness of the Lord is such a special thing.
It cannot be duplicated by any one or anything.

What a joy to know that the goodness of the Lord is what is blessing you so.

No Greater Love

There is no greater love than the love that you have for me
No greater gift than the gift that you gave on Cavalry.

This is why my life is not the same
I am a brand new girl with a brand new name.

So I will lift up my hands and give you praise
I will open up my mouth and sing your holy name.

Oh how great is the love of the Lord
He is the source of the joy that is in my heart.

No greater love in life will I ever no, no greater peace is what I want the world to know.

There is no greater love than God you see
There is no greater God in this whole universe then He.

It's My Time

It's my time
Yes, God said it was.

I have heard from heaven above, for all those things that
you have been through God said it is your time now; he
is going to bless you.

You have put in your time
You have passed the test
And God said get ready now, it's your time to be blessed.

It's my time
Yes, I must confess there were times when I was just a
spiritual mass.

Then God stepped in and the healing began He has
moved those things that were once in control. He told
me to stand and to be bold.

It's my time
I can feel it all around.

I am flying higher than a bird in the sky, just gliding on
the Word.

It's my time
And you need to know
Anything that is standing in my way has got to go.

I am moving like never before
Because it's my time, and God wants the world to know
That trusting in Him is the only way to go.

Expectation

I have great expectation in my God
I expect more than what the world could every know; I expect to prosperous in my soul.

I have great expectation everyday
I expect God to have mercy on me in a mighty way.

I expect to breath in God's fresh air
I expect to have clothes to wear.

I expect to see my family, and close friends
I expect God to cover them.

I expect that all is well
and I don't expect to go to hell.

Expectation can be a wonderful thing when you are expecting to serve God as your Lord and King.

Good Morning

Good morning, Jesus, how are you today?

Good morning, Jesus, would you come and be with me today?

Good morning, Jesus, would you come in my life to stay?

Good morning, Jesus, come and let me hear what your will is for me today.

I love you, Jesus, and need you in a mighty way.

So come on, Jesus, have a seat. I want to hear what you have to say.

Without your guidance, I will not be able to make it in this world today.

So good morning Jesus and let me just say, I love you Jesus and I am thankful for another day.

Turning the Corner

It is just a few steps more if I press on
I know I will make it through the door.

This walk has been a long time coming
If I just hold on I know my turn is coming.

This turn means a great deal to me
It means I have followed God's word, you see.

Turning this corner cannot come soon enough
Because the devil has fought with me for every step.

I can hear God saying, "Press on, my child, don't stop now, it is just around the corner. It is just around the bend, hold your hand out and I'll bring you in."

Sometimes

Sometimes I wonder about my heart it acts as if it does not know the Lord.

Sometimes I just do not understand even though I know God's got a plan.

Sometimes I just don't care
I just want things to be fair.

Sometimes I want to escape

I can't seem to find my place.

Sometimes I have to cry
it seems like my life is a lie.

Sometimes I am too wore down to be strong
I just wish life would leave me alone.

Sometimes I do not want to go home
I just want someone to talk to and lean on.

Sometimes I come and sometimes I go
But, God almighty is the something
who is in all the sometimes that loves me so, and He will never let me go.

You Can Win

I am in a place in my life where everything that I know to be right seems to be out of sight.

I do not understand how this can be when people without morals seem to be blessed more than me.

How can things be so hard for someone like me, when all I want to do is please God, you see?

The enemy seems to have the upper hand, always out to hinder my plans.

Tampering with my lifestyle and with my plans, trying to stop me from saying amen.

But nothing that he throws at me will stop me from getting on my knees.

I am going to praise God no matter what, because it is in Him that I put my trust.

So, if life seems to be overwhelming you too, just stop where you are and do as I do.

Throw up your hands and give God your praise, making sure you bless God's Holy Name.

Choose

Hope with all hope
Press against every pull

Stand up between each fall
Tell the tale behind the truth

Be confident in your tears, try not to worry and draw into fear
Encourage a life by the way you live

Pray for insight and learn how to give
Make the best out of each day then look for God to show you the way

Give help to those in need
To stay strong you must stay on your knees

To have hope you must believe that Jesus Christ did it all, you see.

You Are Special

This is a special time in my life,
God is taking me to brand new heights.

He is doing things so quickly
I have to wonder, does He really want to use me?

I have prayed for this day to tell the world
That God has truly blessed this girl.

He is the mighty force in all things that are great.

Nothing and no one can every take His place.

He is the great I am and the King of Kings, He holds the key to life for all those who believe.

He is the bright and morning star, he is the one who knows your heart.

Give your trust and cares to Him because His love for you will never end for you are special, my friend.

Hope

I'm so glad that my hope is not in man or me, but my hope is in God, you see.

And with his hope I can believe that I have the power to control my own destiny.

This hope keeps me with my head held high because I know hope is waiting on me to take another try.

With this hope I even cry,
And that's okay because I know Jesus is standing by, to wipe away every tear that I cry.

And with this same hope I will take the world on.

By letting them know that Jesus is the only one that can heal their heart, minds bodies, and souls.

All they need to do is let Him have complete control.

I really hope to change a heart today,
just by letting my hope shine in a mighty way.

You see, hope is such a precious gift,
it is so important for you to know what to do with it.

Now I hope you understand
that hope has always been apart of God's master plan.

Because God said, hope is of Him and not of man and it is His hope to see you again.

PIECE THREE

Spiritual Poems for Life

LETTING THE GOOD LORD BE
THANK YOU GOD

Spiritual Poems for Life

Holding On!..97
Wake Up!..98
God, Where Are You?..99
Journey...101
Mirror..102
Chris and Michael...103
Intimacy..104
What Can I Do for You Today, Lord?........................104
I Wonder...106
So, You're Saved?..106
Take the Train..107
My Life..108
Oh, Lord..108
God, Help Us!...109
It's a Mind Thing...110
Love at First Sight..111
Blessed To Be A Blessing..112
Thank You, God...113

Holding On!

I'm holding on with all my might. I'm so tired of this fight!

I find myself crying all through the night, feeling as if there's no hope in sight. So I toss. I turn. I yearn for this pain to go away. But still it stays it has beaten me yet another day.

I won't give up; I won't give in. I'll turn this thing around, I've got to win.

I ask God to help me please;; I've done all that I can do. It just doesn't seem like I can feel you. I speak your words into existence only to find strong resistance.

I ask myself, "How could this be out of all the things you have taught me?"

But this one thing stands true you see, your word is forever and you love me.

So I ask myself, "Who is holding the winning hand and who has always made it possible for me to stand?"

It's God, almighty. He has the master plan.
All I need to do is take a stand and take hold of all God's promises, and believe in His plan.

I know that sometimes things get too rough, the burden seems too heavy and the going gets to be tough. But I'll take this time to give God the praise, for He is making yet another way for me to reach higher heights and to walk out the plans for my life.

Although, it seems there's no one I can trust to understand my hurts, my doubts, and even my disgust—

friends are few and my family is still trying to figure me out.

But I'll hold on.

I'm holding on with all my might!

I can't give up, I can't give in, for God has granted me the Victory I must walk in.

Wake Up!

I wish that I could explain the things that I feel;

I wake up sometimes wondering is this for real?

I just spent the day talking about how I am too blessed to be stressed, and within hours, I am a mess.

God I know that is not of you.

It is that damn devil trying to get through, but he needs to know, "that just will not do"

I am not the same girl he once knew.

Because God has begun a new thing in me-I, see things so differently.

I know the power that I possess, I am a queen of the highest God; I have the power to bless.

I speak those things that I want to exist, exhorting the power of the gifts, the gifts that God left with me - of power and might, not of fear, you see.

My God Jehovah has taught me that you have no power; only the power to deceive and when you speak it's only make-believe. He told me about how you go to and fro trying to make people think that you are in control.

You might be able to use that with someone else, but don't you try that here because I already know I'm blessed.

Yes, I'm mad. I'm mad as hell.

All those years before you were setting me up to fail, trying to take what was rightfully mine; Lord knows you have got to be out of your mind.

You tried your best to kill me too, but God Almighty knew you would lose. You should have done it when you had the chance. It's too late now. I have taken a stand.

I made the choice in my life I want to live for Jesus Christ, and do what is right.

I will serve Him with all my heart and soul. I'll speak His truth and be bold, and I'll let the world know that Jesus Christ saves souls.

I hope I have explained just how I feel, I woke up!

God is real.

God, Where Are You?

God, where are you? I asked. And this was His reply:

I am everywhere.

I am here, I am there, I am with you even when you are feeling despair.

I am the wind that you see blowing all the leaves.
I am the birds that fly in the sky; I am the fish in the sea,

I am the air that you breathe, I am the sight in all you see.

Everywhere you look, you should see me.

I am the mountain and the sky.

I am the sparkle in every baby's eye.

I am the rain that falls from the sky; I am that perfect cloud way up high.

I am the stars the sun and the moon; I am even known as a monsoon.

I am the winter, spring, the summer and the fall.

I am the first, the last, the beginning and end of it all.

So, you ask where I am?

I am the catch in your fall.

I am the one who uncovers it all.

I am the hope in your hope.

I am the only one that can boast.

I am everything and all that is in between.

My children know me as the King of Kings and they depend on me for every, and all things.

Where am I?

You tell me!

Journey

I want to tell you about me:
I am a young woman in my forties, you see.

I made my mind up that it was time for me to find out what it was like to be free.

Free from life's bondages, because they were just killing me.
And so, I started out on this journey to find the God in me.

I never knew just where this journey would take me, but it has taken me to places where I didn't want to be.

This thing has made me look at me and it was not a pretty sight. I really didn't want to see. But because I've chosen to be free, I had to sit down and take a good look at me.

I found out that most of my problems started with me. And when I stopped blaming others for my inadequacy, things began to change, please believe me.

I had to learn how to live and how to let go.
And how to believe that God is always in control.

Yes, this journey is taking me places where I didn't want to be.

I'm losing loved ones and friends aren't what they seem to be. This thing is really hard on me, but I have chosen to take this journey, you see.

There is no doubt in my mind that I've got to be free. I won't turn back! I won't get off track! I'll walk this thing out; you can count on that.

I'll push, I'll press, and yes, I'll even get upset.

But the God in me won't let me be stressed.

He has made it clear that He has given me His best and it's up to me to do the rest.

So, I'll go on this journey with great pride, knowing that God is on my side. The doors that he has opened no man can shut.

He has gone before me and all my needs have been met. Yes, this journey I am taking is for me, God ordained it from the foundation of the world just for me.

Now, if you are on life's journey like me, take this advice, it's free.

Always let God be your guide.
Never ever put Him to the side.

Throw away all of your foolish pride and give God your very best, then just stand back and watch Him bless.

Mirror

In the mirror of life, how can you explain your sight?

What do you see when your eyes look through the mirror and see that person you have come to be?

Can you look at yourself and feel proud and pleased, knowing that you are not the same person you used to be?

Can you take pride in knowing that maybe someone might be able to model his or her life from this same sight?

In the mirror of life, what do you see? Do you see hope, love, and life in the way God planned it to be? Have you taken the time to investigate some of the blemishes you see?

When looking in the mirror one can only see what's on the surface.

So pleased don't be deceived, it's not always easy to see. but, I've come to prescribe a cure for you.

The name of this medicine is **Jesus.**

Take as much of Him as you need. You ask the cost? Well, it's free.

Chris and Michael

Christopher and Michael are their names. Both are my brothers I need to explain, they're no longer with us now, for God has called them to take a bow. Yet, it still seems strange because I want to call their names.

And even though I know they're much better off, the void in my heart makes me mourn their loss. I still wish that they were here. I want to hold them close and keep them near. They had laughs like no others, they were special, they're my brothers.

Although we cannot change time, they will forever be on my mind. I ask God to give me peace, for I know they are just asleep. And in due time we will meet again, but this time it will never end.

Love,
Teresa

Intimacy

What does it mean to have intimacy with God to me?

It means being as close as close as one can be.
It means I can speak for Him and He speaks for me.

It means that when you look at me He seems to appear, in the way that I talk and give a listening ear, you know He is near.

It means I can tell Him anything at anytime, because He has my best interests in mind.

It means He is my friend through thick and thin. It means we share and he cares about every, and all things.

Intimacy with God you see, is like living inside one skin. The colors may vary, but He lives within.

What Can I Do for You Today, Lord?

What can I do? What can I say? How can I show you I love you today?

I'll watch what I do, I'll watch what I say, and hopefully, I'll make it clear to someone today that you are the only way.

I'll magnify my God given gifts, so when people look at me they will know you exist. I won't just talk about what you have done, but I'll ask them are they ready for you to come?

I place my life in your hand, I want to be at your command.

Teach me how to serve you Lord! I want to do all I can.

What can I do for you today? Would you like for me to call up someone and say, "God loves
you and have a blessed day?"

Or when passing by someone (today) I'll smile when I look his or her way and remind him or her it's just a great day.

I don't want to miss this chance to do something God for you.
Lord, you have blessed me in so many ways.

I cannot go on another day without showing my appreciation I want to give you true dedication.

After all, it was because of your many revelations that I have the mind to live and love without hesitation. Lord, you give me so much inspiration.

So, I need to know, what I can do for you Lord to help make your day?

Put it in my heart and I'll get on it right away.

I promise to give you my very best knowing in life, though I know there are many tests.

I hope in some way I'll please you today, for I don't want it any other way.

I just need to know what can I do for you today?

I Wonder

I wonder what God sees when He looks at you and when He looks at me.

I wonder if He's proud of the people we have come to be.

I wonder if He can call on us to walk out the plans for His land. I wonder if we can be fair and just to every woman or man no matter what? I wonder if we can set the captives free, by spreading God's word in unity.

It's our duty, you see.

I wonder when the world looks at us, do they see the image of God or just us?

I wonder when God looks at us, is He really pleased or filled with disgust?

I wonder, I wonder, I wonder about a lot of things, but mostly I wonder why God still loves me.

So, You're Saved?

So you're saved is what you are telling me, your life has changed, you live differently?

Your walk with God has set you free, you say come look at me, I am the picture of true liberty.

So you're saved well let me see, can I tell the difference between you and me?

When you speak words out of your mouth will they bring forth hope or just more doubt?

And if I called on you in need of prayer, would you stop what you were doing because you care?

So you're saved?
Oh, I can tell by the way you carry yourself.
You wear it well.

Take the Train

It was my first train ride. What a great surprise, as I watched the landscape while the train passed by.
It's like looking at pictures from a book quickly before the pages flip.

Yes, my first train ride as I watched out the window in great surprise, just to sit back and see the land when looking at it, I saw God's hands. I saw everything He had touched from the breeze in the air to the settling of the dust.

How He used the earth like a canvas.

He painted the land with the wave of his hand. How he spoke to the seeds and made the trees grow and when He winked his eye, the rivers began to flow.
With each wildflower that he designed, He had all his children in mind.

Not one would be the same, each one unique with a different color and a different name.
Yes, my first train ride, and what a surprise it has brought me closer to God and I thank Him for the ride.

My Life

When I think about life and what it means to live, to love, to share, and to have wonderful dreams, I thank God for all these things.

I try to live each day with a smile and I hope, and pray to bless someone throughout the day. I know when I bless someone you see God is delighted with me and just to think that I could put a smile on God's face makes my heart race and takes my mind to another place.

I want to live my life you see to please God for he has been so good to me. He's taking me to higher heights;; He's turned my wrongs into rights. He has given me another chance in life and I want to make sure I get it right.

So I'll take this time, you see, to read my Bible and study diligently and speak God's word over my life by doing this I know things will be all right.

So I'll take each day and think about life and just maybe I'll get it right.

Oh, Lord

Oh, Lord, make known to me the purpose for my life.

Oh, Lord.
Give a place in my heart to feel your might.

I need your presence in my life. Without you, I am unable to fight. Unable to fight against the powers that be, I need your help, come be with me.

Teach me your will, teach me your way;; I'll put to practice all that you say.

I'll slay the devil with your words and it will be known that he heard, because when the people look at me they'll know the King of Kings lives within me.

Oh, Lord, make known the purpose for my life, so I can stay focused and do what's right.

I want to give you lots of praise!

I need to please you every day, and if I don't, just let me say,

Oh Lord, forgive me each and every day.

God, Help Us!

It seems strange how we who are called by your name expect great change without doing anything. God, help us!

When will the day come when we will act like your son the one who gave of himself just so we all could be blessed? Lord I pray for the day when we begin making our own way, not leaning on man, but taking hold of your hand, and doing all the things that you plan.

God, help us!
It breaks my heart to see just how irresponsible we can be-

Missing the mark on life so freely. After all you have done how could this be?

God, help us!

We live our lives so recklessly, not caring about what our children see, this is not the way it should be.

God, help us please!
We're destroying their lives before they begin, we are taking away their hope and this is a sin.

God, help us!
I wonder how things would be if we took the time to achieve our true destiny? And live our lives the way God has planned, becoming the women and men who will bless the land.

God, help us to stand and be bold, knowing that you are in control!

We need you so desperately, God, help us please!
Without your guidance, we will never succeed.

It's a Mind Thing

Let's take a flight, go beyond the walls of your mind, and find yourself in a different time; a time before the world, as you have known, a time before Jesus decided he would leave His throne.

He did come, and set the captives free. To give them back what the devil thought he could take away so easily.

It was life, what a great mistake, God had to put him in his place.

Now just think about this wonderful deed, and then tell me why and how we still act so irresponsibly.

God has given us life as kings and queens and yet we live like possessed fiends.

Taking everything to the extreme, never knowing the true value of life and the honor it brings.

To those who live their life for the King of Kings who has all power, and controls all and everything

Let's take a flight. Pass the walls of your mind and tap into the great divine mystery that God left for you to find, to tell you about life's great rewards when you truly serve the Lord.

How your every need has already been met and no demon in hell can stop that. How His blood has set you free and He's all you will ever need.

Come take a hold of this vision with me and see how life is really supposed to be when born under a new name, a child of the most high God, Jesus Christ is the name I claim.

Therefore, the mind is a wonderful thing when you can believe in God's promises His hopes, and dreams.

Love at First Sight

Love at first sight, I know that happened when God saw you and me.

It was love at first sight in spite of all the un-right. He felt we were worth the fight.

Therefore, He left heaven and came to earth and started this great work.

He came and sat in the synagogue where the lessons began.

He had to show them who God really was and tell them it was Him they had been waiting for.

He walked the earth with great dignity teaching the people how to be free.

It is too bad that even then they could not believe after walking right beside Him.

They could not conceive the mighty power that He possesses and they kept trying to put Him to the test.

And even after all of that, the
love at first sight He still possesses.

I come to finish this job you see, my father has assigned it to me, He loves you so dearly.

It was love at first sight can't you see?
From the moment He blew into the dirt, He knew of your worth.

Blessed To Be A Blessing

I am blessed to be a blessing.

I did not always know, I thought they were for me to keep, I did not want to let them go.

But I must release what God has given me if I am to please Him you see, for He has blessed me to be a blessing so all the world can see.

These blessings are bigger than you and me
God ordained it in heaven and assigned them to you as well as to me, to spread them throughout the land to give to every woman, child and man.

Now what you do with your blessing means a lot,
He determines what you may need by the way you give so freely.

Now, pass your blessings on each and every day and allow God to continually bless you in a mighty way.

Thank You, God

(A Prayer)

Thank you, God!

For making it so easy to get to know you

I realize that Jesus made it all possible for me.

I thank you, Jesus, that you died on the cross.

I thank you Jesus, for giving me a choice. I chose you as my Lord and Savior.

Father, I thank you for my requests made known unto you, that you have given me.

I thank you for taking the time, teaching me, and for showing me just what your will is for my life.

You have opened doors in my life that no man will ever be able to shut and I want to thank you.

I thank you for teaching me what love is.

I thank you for your patience with me, for your understanding, and compassion for me.

I thank you that when I feel alone you comfort me.

I thank you when I cry, for you wipe the tears from my eyes. I want to thank you.

Thank you for each passing day, you make it known that you are the Way.

You're my up when I'm down, you're my strength when I'm weak, my hope when I'm hopeless. I want to thank you.

I thank you for teaching me how to pray and always making a way, letting me know that I'm okay.

Thank you for blessings seen and unseen, and for all those things in between.

I lift up your name and give you praise,

I thank you,
I thank you forever and a day.

About the Author

Teresa Johnson is a single mother of one son and grandmother of two beautiful girls, Kayla & Peyton.

A native of St. Louis, Missouri, she is the fifth of six children born to Marvin and Beatrice Johnson.

From 1993-2004 Teresa owned and operated an in home daycare center. It is during that time that she began writing short stories to help teach her children. Teresa is a God fearing woman who loves the Lord. It is through her poems that she tries to show others just how worthy God is to be praised and worshipped. She is the author of the books *Spiritual Poems for Life* and *Just My Thoughts*.

www.ingramcontent.com/pod-product-compliance
Lightning Source LLC
Chambersburg PA
CBHW072053290426
44110CB00014B/1667